The Biology o

MW01290066

Reprogram Your Subconscious Mind for Business Success

Odille Remmert and Steve Remmert

ISBN-13: 978-1721509973
ISBN-10: 1721509976

DEDICATION

We dedicate this book to our Patreon Community and every client we've worked with.

Without each of you, we would not have developed this modality to the extent we have.

Every challenge we've come across has inspired us to find solutions, extra tools, techniques, and new ways of teaching this information.

We also dedicate this publication to each person – in our online meetups and sessions, and in our weekly local meetup group – who has asked questions that have inspired us to write this book.

CONTENTS

Odille Remmert and Steve Remmert

ACKNOWLEDGMENTS

We would like to express a special "Thank You!" to
Robert G. Smith – creator of FasterEFT.
Without him and his modality, we would not have made
the changes we've made to our own lives (including meeting
each other at one of his training seminars)
– and this book would not exist.

Thank you, Robert, for everything you've done, and
continue to do.

We appreciate you.

Odille Remmert and Steve Remmert

Introduction

Forget everything you've ever heard about success – including anything you've heard about the effect your subconscious mind has on your results. What we're going to share with you in this book will probably contradict a lot of what you've heard in the past – and it will certainly challenge your current perceptions. BUT, it will also empower you beyond your expectations. It will give you real control over what you experience, and what you create in your life. In all areas of your life, and in particular, your business and financial experiences.

There are a few points we'd like to make, before we start, that will give you the best foundation from which to absorb the powerful information we have to share with you:

1. As amazing as the information in this book may seem at first, it is based on physiology and science. You do not have to believe in anything, and it doesn't matter what your personal or religious beliefs are. This is about neuroscience rather than the "spiritual" understanding of the subconscious mind.

2. Knowing this information is a great start; however, just reading this book is not going to create success in your business. You will need

to take action and follow the steps we've outlined, to change the subconscious references in order to create the results you're aiming for.

3. You may need to suspend your current understanding of how your mind works, in order to absorb the information. There are scientific references in the "Resources" section, if you need them.

4. While we have given you the information, and we are available (see the resources at the back of this book) to answer your questions, offer guidance, and cheer you on… we, of course, cannot do it for you – this will take determination and action on your part.

5. The nature of the subconscious (as you'll learn in the following chapters) is to keep you safe by keeping you in alignment with what has always been – you're still alive, right? This means that you may experience some resistance to making the changes. That will be your subconscious doing whatever it takes to steer you away from real change, in order to keep you safe. This is when you'll need to use your conscious mind to override those efforts, and push forward anyway. You have nothing to lose, and your goals and dreams to gain!

Above all, it's important (and empowering) to remember that YOU are the boss of you and every moment is a choice – even if it's just a choice of where to put your focus. You decide what your subconscious keeps, and what gets changed. You have more power than you may think! It's time to take the controls.

Odille Remmert and Steve Remmert

The Main Reason
Most Entrepreneurs Fail

There are all kinds of suggestions, courses, information, training, and books out there that explain why most entrepreneurs fail – or why most small businesses don't make it past the first year, or why most people who want to leave their job and do what they love for a living never make the leap… and if they do… you guessed it, most fail.

Failing to build a mailing list; lack of marketing skills or budget; failing to network; not writing a blog; not making enough videos; not creating podcasts; using (or not using) paid advertising on social media; failing to become an "influencer" on social media; overlooking collaboration; procrastinating picking up the phone; resisting taking massive action; not building a brand… and on and on – all of these may have their place, but the truth is – they're symptoms, not the cause.

The main reason most entrepreneurs fail is not because of marketing, or because they're taking the wrong action – or not taking action at all. It's because they have subconscious programming that is either preventing them from taking that action, or is affecting their judgement so that they're taking the wrong action.

Trying to change what you're doing with your business is like cutting the branches off a weed. It will just grow back. You could do everything perfectly... and, as long as you keep the same subconscious programming, you would still end up with the same results you're getting now. When you take the weed out by the root, and replace that root with a plant you really want in your garden, THEN you have made a real change. When you change the subconscious programming that is determining your actions/inaction; decisions; perception; judgement; motivation; creativity; ability to communicate; productivity; and everything else – THEN your success is automatic.

Regardless of what seems to be the problem for you right now – whether you're trying to get a business going, struggling with an existing business, or dream of making a living doing what you love – the first step is realizing that it's not about what's happening now... it's about what your subconscious is holding from the past as "proof" of who you are, and how the world works. And the great news is – you can change it! You can't change the actual past, of course, but you can change the effects of it – you can change how that data is held in your subconscious – and therefore, how it determines the results you create, moving forward.

How the Subconscious Mind Works

From birth, the subconscious is interpreting and recording experiences. It doesn't record experiences as they happen, accurately, as a camera would – it interprets the experience, filtering it through the information collected from previous experiences, gives it meaning, and then files that data as "evidence". This data forms the foundation that supports beliefs – that proves beliefs!

For example, an experience of being abandoned may be interpreted (depending on the data collected from previous experiences) by the subconscious to mean: "I'm not worthy" or "I'm not loveable" or "I don't deserve love". When that child experiences a bully at school, the experience with the bully is filtered through the existing data that supports the "I'm not worthy" structure of belief, and is added to it as further proof of that "fact".

As the "evidence" increases, the structure becomes stronger, and the adult that child becomes may suffer from social anxiety, lack of confidence and low self-esteem. Every venture he attempts in the business world will be filtered through that "fact" (supported by the proof in the form of subconscious childhood memories) that "I'm not worthy". No matter how hard he tries to build a mailing list, or what he does with social media and marketing, the feelings of not being worthy will affect his efforts and his results.

How the Subconscious Mind Controls the Conscious Mind

In every moment, the subconscious is referring to the data it holds (in the form of subconscious childhood memories), then prompting the brain to trigger the organs to produce chemicals. These chemicals create sensations, emotions, feelings, and impulses. The conscious mind then interprets these sensations, and behaves accordingly. So, we think that we are making decisions and choices consciously; we think that we are choosing our thoughts, using our logic and reasoning – but, the truth is: the subconscious is controlling the conscious mind through sensations, emotions, feelings, and impulses in the body, based on what it holds as "evidence" of who we are and how the world works.

Staying Safe

The primary role of the subconscious is to keep you safe. It will do whatever it takes to keep you safe. And staying safe means staying the same. (You're still alive, right?). It also means staying in alignment with your "tribe". Since humans are not designed to live solo, belonging to the "tribe" is a core instinct. In particular, children are designed with a primary drive to please those who are raising them – to avoid being abandoned. To the subconscious, abandonment means death. Staying in alignment with your "tribe" equals survival.

If you grew up in a household where rich people were disapproved of, your subconscious may (depending on the rest of the data) have linked having money with being disapproved of by your family. And since being disapproved of equals a danger of being rejected – which, in turn equals "death" according to that survival instinct – your subconscious will be doing whatever it can to keep you from ending up with more than a certain amount of money. Of course, it makes no logical sense... but the subconscious has no ability to use logic or reason; that's the conscious mind's job. The subconscious is operating purely from programming, and linking information – whether it makes sense to the conscious mind or not.

You may find that you lack the motivation to take certain action – even though you know it's what you need to do, in order to make more money. Your subconscious, in this case, is referring to the "fact" that having more money is dangerous, and then prompting your brain and body to produce chemicals that cause you to feel doubt, or laziness, or resistance, or tiredness, or ill, or ... whatever it takes to stop you from moving forward towards the "danger" of being out of alignment with your "tribe".

You may find that every opportunity you choose turns out to be a scam; or every time you think about making that video, or writing that blog, you are filled with doubt that anyone would be interested in hearing what you have to say.

Behind the scenes, your subconscious is prompting your brain and body to produce chemicals that cause the feelings and sensations that your conscious mind is interpreting as doubt. Your conscious mind then finds reasons for that doubt. The conscious mind's job is to make sense of experiences. The conscious mind uses logic and reason to make sense of the world, and to make sense of experiences. So, you'll find yourself coming up with what seem like perfectly valid reasons for not doing what you need to do in order to achieve what you want to achieve.

Jane's Story

A client of ours (who we'll call Jane), who invests in the stock exchange, found that, despite knowing that she was using a system through which others were making money, she was consistently losing money. When she should have sold, she was delaying until it was too late. When she should have held onto a stock, she was trigger-happy, and sold before the stock climbed.

Through the process we share with you in this book, we discovered a few childhood memories that provided "proof" that she was "stupid". There were a few experiences with her father calling her stupid, and a couple of school memories where she felt stupid. The combination of whatever other references her subconscious held – through which these "stupid" experiences were filtered – resulted in a core belief that she was stupid.

What's the connection? Jane's subconscious was constantly referring to the "evidence" that proves that "stupid" was who she was (it's a fact – here's the proof!). And then prompting her brain and body to produce chemicals that would affect her decisions, judgement, and actions, to guide her towards experiencing being stupid. So, in the case of the day-trading – she was using a system that was working for others; so, as far as her subconscious was concerned, there was a "danger" of her succeeding – which would not be in alignment with "stupid".

Therefore, whenever she knew, intellectually that, according to the system, she should hold onto a stock, her subconscious prompted her brain and body to produce chemicals that caused feelings of nervousness or anxiety. Her conscious mind, recognizing these sensations, would immediately find reasons for them – "It's going to go down. I'll lose money. I've lost so much already. I daren't take the chance" and "My gut instinct is to sell". And so, she would sell... and the stock would continue to climb.

When, according to the system she was following – and trusted – she should sell, her subconscious would prompt her brain and body to produce feelings of fear and apprehension – which her conscious mind reasoned: "But what if it goes up? Last time, it went up. I always miss out. I'd better hold on to it." – and of course, the stock would drop. In this way, Jane was constantly able to compare herself to the others who were making money using the same system – and feel the familiar feeling of "stupid".

Once we changed those childhood memories to the opposite – Jane's father telling her that he's proud of her; Jane's teachers praising her; and so on – she no longer felt those stress feelings when trading. And she was able to use her intellect and her knowledge to make decisions, instead of being controlled by her fear. Now, her subconscious is doing whatever it takes to keep her in alignment with the NEW "evidence" – that she's clever, worthy, and deserving.

The Direct Link
Between Your Emotions and
Your Business Results

You've probably heard that stress can have an effect on your life. You may also have heard that emotions can affect your outlook, and even your decisions… but how? Here's exactly how emotions not only affect your business results – but <u>determine</u> them!

What Are Emotions?

Emotions appear to be intangible and "ethereal", but they are in fact simply sensations in the body caused by chemicals. These chemicals are produced by your own brain and body, and they can have a powerful effect on your physiology.

The Physiological Effect of Emotions

The emergency "fight-freeze-flight" state is caused by stress chemicals that impact heart rate, blood flow, and various other biological processes. Any negative emotion is a level of this state, and during the fight-freeze-flight state: blood is pumped away from the organs, to the extremities - in preparation for running away or fighting; digestion, healing, and any other systems that are not essential for surviving immediate danger in the short-term, are reduced or shut down.

Cells switch from "growth" to "protection" mode; and – most importantly for the topic of business – blood is drained from the prefrontal cortex of the brain (where you do your cognitive thinking: problem solving; processing of information; strategizing; and other "higher" forms of thinking) – which means you are unable to think as clearly or make decisions as effectively.

The brain and body don't know the difference between reality and imagination. You'll notice, when you watch a movie, your body reacts as if the movie is real – increased heart-rate, boost of adrenaline, and other physiological changes. This means that the danger does not need to be real for your body and brain to go into the emergency fight-freeze-flight state.

How Emotions Impact Business Decisions, Productivity, and Creativity

When you are feeling any kind of negative emotion, you are in a level of the fight-freeze-flight stress state. With the prefrontal cortex of your brain effectively "offline" you are literally unable to think straight. You are less able to notice opportunities and solutions; your judgement is impaired; and your communication skills are affected. In addition to this, your creativity and productivity are impacted – since it is not necessary to be creative or productive when you are in immediate physical danger.

"But I Work Best Under Pressure!"

This is a common misperception. If you find that you work best under pressure, it is more likely that you "work" under pressure. In other words, you need to feel pressure, in order to do the work in the first place, rather than being more effective or doing a better job under pressure. "I work better under pressure" is a belief based on subconscious programming supported by "evidence" in the form of memories.

If you were to change that "evidence", you would find yourself happy and motivated to work without needing the pressure. And in fact, with your prefrontal cortex fully online, you would be more efficient, more creative, and more productive. So, if you think you're doing a good job under pressure – without the full use of your cognitive thinking – imagine what you can do, with that part of your brain fully functional!

How Emotions Impact Motivation, Communication, and Action

As we mentioned before, when you're feeling any kind of negative emotion, you're in a level of the "fight-freeze-flight" emergency state. And while you're in that emergency state, the cells of your brain and body are in "protection mode" instead of "growth mode" – they're not receiving nutrients as effectively. Your organs are not receiving the blood-flow they need, and various other systems are in "emergency mode". This, naturally, affects your ability to feel motivated and energetic.

With the prefrontal cortex of your brain impaired, you're also less effective in your communication, your ability to plan and strategize, and you are likely to feel "lazy" and tired – creating a resistance to taking action.

This is how your subconscious controls your conscious perception, decisions, choices, and actions – in order to keep you "safe" by keeping you the same and in alignment with your "tribe". And this is why it's so difficult to change habits and to get yourself to move forward in new directions. It's a matter of survival, as far as the subconscious is concerned. And survival will override desire!

Think of your subconscious as a burglar-alarm that is going off when there's no reason. Either it's faulty, or it goes off when the cat moves. No amount of talking to it, or reasoning with it is going to convince it that there's no reason to activate when the cat moves – or when the wind blows. You need to reprogram it.

Your subconscious is the same. Another way to think of it is like the autopilot in an airplane. As the pilot, you can't push the plane physically, and no amount of repeating the new instructions as affirmations is going to change the course of the flight. And certainly, getting frustrated with the current path won't change it. You need to simply change the coordinates in the autopilot. And then, the aircraft will automatically head in the new direction – no effort or willpower required.

When you change the "coordinates" in your subconscious, you will find yourself automatically experiencing new perception, new perspective, making different decisions, feeling motivated, being creative and productive, and taking different action. No effort or willpower required. It will be natural and automatic.

Odille Remmert and Steve Remmert

How the Subconscious is Programmed

There's no magic or mystery about how the subconscious is programmed. It simply collects and connects data from experiences. This data forms the "evidence" that supports the structures of subconscious beliefs. Every new experience is filtered through the structures built of the data from previous experiences, and then that information added to the existing structure – forming a unique version of reality. This is how we learn who we are and how the world works. It's why a baby can be born in rural Africa or Hollywood, and learn to fit in, and survive in that environment.

It's Not Like a Camera

Although the subconscious collects data from experiences, it does not record experiences accurately, as they happen, the way a camera would. It interprets the experience, based on whatever data it already holds, assigns meaning, and then adds that to the rest of the data. In other words, memories are not an accurate record of events.

The Nature of Memories

Neuroscience has discovered that memories are not stored as complete records in the brain. In fact, every time we recall a memory, the data is pieced together as we recall it. In addition to this, as a memory is reconstructed each time it is recalled, it is also adjusted and changed according to experiences that have occurred since that particular event. Not only are memories not accurate, but they also change every time we recall them.

There Are No "Memories" in Your Brain

There are no pictures in your brain. There are no sounds, there are no feelings, and there are certainly no people in your brain. There are only neurons (nerve cells) and chemicals in there! When you recall a memory, all that's happening are connections between neurons in specific sequences, which trigger a release of chemicals that cause sensations we recognize as emotions and feelings. This is great news – because it means that you can change the way those neurons are firing. You can change your memories – which will, in turn, change the references your subconscious is referring to as "proof" and "evidence" of who you are and how the world works. And that means, you can change the automatic results you experience in your life. You can literally redesign yourself to achieve what you want to achieve.

For example: If you have lack of self-confidence, you can find the memories that provide the "proof" that supports the reasons for that lack of confidence, and you can change them to the opposite. Since the subconscious cannot tell the difference between reality and imagination, and will believe whatever you give it – it will then be referring to the new "evidence" that provides the "proof" for self-confidence. It will come naturally and automatically.

Michael's Story:

Michael wanted to build his business. He'd heard that developing a strong presence on social media was essential to business success for his niche; but every time he thought about posting in social media, or even writing a blog, he felt a strong resistance. He put it off for months, and just assumed it was because he wasn't "a writer". He even tried outsourcing his social media. He paid someone to post regularly for him. But that didn't seem to work at all. It seemed that no-one was interested in what he had to offer.

Using what we're going to share with you later in this book, Michael found childhood memories from when he was in 3rd grade that were supporting a subconscious belief. His teacher was an angry, impatient woman who never seemed satisfied with what he did. He had a couple of memories of being humiliated in front of the class for work he thought he'd done well. Those experiences, filtered through whatever data was already stored in his subconscious from previous experiences, were providing "proof" that it was dangerous to create something for others to read. Remember: The subconscious doesn't know the difference between reality and imagination, and cannot use logic or reason. In addition to this, humiliation is a stress state – a level of the emergency fight-freeze-flight state – which equates to "danger" as far as the subconscious is concerned.

So, every time Michael considered writing a post for others to read, his subconscious was referring to the data stored from those early experiences – the connection between: others reading what he's written, and "danger" – and then prompting his brain and body to produce chemicals that created the sensations of laziness, tiredness, and resistance. In addition, it shut down his prefrontal cortex so that he couldn't think of what to write. It was doing whatever it took to "protect" him from the danger. Note: This was all happening "in the background" – without his conscious awareness.

Michael changed those memories – to the teacher praising him because his work was so advanced for his age, and sending a letter home to his parents, telling them how proud they should be of their son – then, whenever Michael thought about writing a social media or blog post, his subconscious referred to the new "evidence" that proved it was not only safe to write, but that it was rewarding. And it then prompted his brain and body to produce chemicals that created feelings of excitement and anticipation – so that Michael found that he couldn't wait to write, and he actually enjoyed it.

Of course, since he was no longer in the emergency stress state, the prefrontal cortex of his brain was fully engaged; so, not only was he enjoying writing – he was good at it too! And he was able to start building a following due to his witty and useful posts.

Odille Remmert and Steve Remmert

How Your Childhood Affects Your Business

It may seem absurd, at first, but – as far away as your childhood may seem from what you're doing today – as mentioned in previous chapters, it is providing the "evidence" that "proves" your subconscious beliefs. And it is your subconscious beliefs that provide the structure for who you are and how the world works.

References, Evidence, and Beliefs

Subconscious beliefs are supported by "evidence" that proves them. This evidence is collected and organized by the subconscious mind, based on whatever evidence already exists – from previous experiences. As we experience, the subconscious refers to the existing structure of beliefs, based on evidence collected from previous experiences, and applies those "facts" – or filters the new experience through that information – and then determines what the new experience means, based on that information. It then adds the new information to the existing data for future reference.

For example: If you feel overwhelmed by any area of your business, although it seems to be the current experience that is overwhelming, it is in fact the reference in your subconscious (in the form of childhood memories) that is causing the overwhelm.

Feeling overwhelmed is the result of stress chemicals in your blood-stream and the act of trying to use the prefrontal cortex of your brain while it is offline (as part of the fight-freeze-flight stress state). Getting into a calm physiological state brings the prefrontal cortex of your brain back online – which reinstates your cognitive thinking, which, in turn, reduces the feeling of overwhelm.

So, what's causing the stress chemicals? Your subconscious is referring to the records it holds (in the form of childhood memories), then prompting your brain to trigger your organs to produce the fight-freeze-flight chemicals. Trying to force yourself to take action in those areas of your business that feel overwhelming will only increase the level of stress chemicals in your blood stream.

You could use relaxation techniques to calm your system down to the point where your prefrontal cortex is back online – and that may work temporarily – but, as long as your subconscious holds "proof" that you're "in danger", it will continue to trigger your "burglar alarm" in an effort to keep you safe.

If you change whatever "evidence" the subconscious holds (change those childhood memories), it will no longer be triggering the fight-freeze-flight response. Which means, you will no longer go into that stress state; your prefrontal cortex will remain active and working optimally; and you will be able to think strategically, come up with solutions, organize, process information, and deal with that area of your business in a productive, creative, proactive way.

Fear of Asking for Payment

Before I (Odille here) found this information, I hated charging people for work I did. I hated asking to be paid, and I hated reminding people if they hadn't paid me. As a professional singer, I would do a gig, and then not want to ask to be paid. I would sit around and wait – hoping the person who booked me would come over to me with the payment. If they didn't, I would have to force myself to go over to them and ask for the payment (cringing internally, as I did so). I would go into a freeze-flight state when I had to invoice the clients I was writing for as a professional writer. I could feel the adrenaline pumping through my bloodstream as I thought about sending an invoice.

The amazing thing is, it felt like once I invoiced, they wouldn't pay me. Of course, that's illogical because if I didn't invoice, I certainly wasn't going to get paid! But my conscious mind reasoned that it was because I had had experiences in the past of people not paying me. Naturally, I still had to invoice people… and so I would, in a state of anxiety and fear, make myself send the invoice, and then feel that fear and anxiety every time I thought about it… followed by immense relief (and surprise) when the payment did arrive.

What was going on in the background is fascinating – and a great example of how the subconscious is controlling the conscious mind through the body, based on childhood memories, without the conscious mind's awareness:

Using the process we'll share with you later in this book, I found a memory I had completely forgotten about, consciously. Up until that day, I hadn't recalled it at all! I suddenly remembered that, in my family, we were raised with the understanding that: "If you ask, you don't get!" It was a politeness/manners thing. "You wait to be offered. It's rude to ask." It was being installed along the lines of learning to say "please" and "thank-you". "Now that you've asked, you can't have it. You wait to be offered." This is one thing if you're trying to teach children manners… but it is completely impractical as an adult, of course! Well, it's impractical as a child as well.…

Of course, not all children will process these experiences in the same way – it will depend on what structures of "evidence" have already been created in the subconscious, through which these experiences are now being filtered. In my case, every time I needed to ask to be paid, or invoice someone, my subconscious (without my conscious awareness) was referring to the "fact" that if I ask, I don't get. It was then prompting my brain and body to produce stress chemicals, putting me into the emergency "fight-freeze-flight" state - to keep me "safe" by trying to prevent me from asking... and therefore "saving" me from not getting.

As illogical as it is to the conscious mind to not ask in order to receive, the subconscious has no ability to use logic or reason, and, like a computer, will simply go by whatever it's programmed with.

So, I used Childhood Memory Transformation (CMT) therapy (which we will share with you later in this book) to change that reference – that "evidence" held in my subconscious that "proved" that asking for something results in not receiving it. And, I was then able to invoice, ask for payment, and charge people for my services and products, without any sign of fear, anxiety or stress. My subconscious no longer has a reference that asking is dangerous, so it no longer prompts the stress response!

Odille Remmert and Steve Remmert

The Conscious Mind vs The Subconscious Mind

Understanding the differences between the subconscious and the conscious mind is a key part of being able to reprogram your subconscious mind for business success. It is the differences between the two that make it possible to achieve this kind of control over your results.

Conscious Mind	Subconscious Mind
primary role - to make sense of experiences	primary role - to keep you alive
uses logic and reason to make sense of the world	operates solely from "evidence" it holds (in the form of data from childhood memories).
able to determine reality from imagination	cannot determine the difference between reality and imagination
uses logic and reason to judge something as "unrealistic"	will believe whatever it's given – as long as it does not hold "evidence" (in the form of childhood memories) that contradict the new "evidence".
can look at a family pattern such as violence or poverty, and know that it is undesirable	holds "evidence" that "proves" that in order to fit in with the "tribe" (i.e. survival) it is crucial to maintain the pattern of violence or poverty.

The Main Differences Between the Conscious Mind and the Subconscious Mind Are:

- The primary role of the conscious mind is to make sense of experiences; the primary role of the subconscious is to keep you alive.

- The conscious mind uses logic and reason to make sense of the world; the subconscious operates purely according to the "evidence" it holds (in the form of data from memories).

- The conscious mind is able to determine reality from imagination; the subconscious cannot tell the difference between reality and imagination. An example of this is: When you think about something you fear, you can feel the feeling of fear without being in danger "in reality". When you think of something you love, you can feel the feeling of it, without it happening in this moment. As you think of something, the connection between neurons in the neocortex of your brain triggers the release of matching chemicals – that provide the feelings, emotions, sensations, and impulses that would be produced if the event were occurring in reality. Another example of this is watching a scary movie – your body goes into the same fight-freeze-flight response it would if you were in real danger, while your conscious mind

29

knows it's just a movie.

- The conscious mind is able to use logic and reason to judge something as "unrealistic"; the subconscious does not have this ability, and will believe whatever it's given – as long as it does not hold "evidence" (in the form of childhood memories) that contradict the new "evidence".

- The conscious mind can look at a family pattern of violence or poverty, and know that it is undesirable; the subconscious holds "evidence" that "proves" that in order to fit in with the "tribe" (which, evolutionarily, is essential for survival) it is crucial to maintain the pattern of violence or poverty. To stray too far from those patterns risks rejection from the "tribe", and therefore "death".

Remember, the subconscious has no ability to reason or use logic. It is simply operating according to the programming – just as a computer does. To change it, you need to change the programming, rather than attempt to use reason or logic the way the conscious mind does.

Can Memories Really Be Changed?

Not only *can* memories be changed – they are *already* being changed, every time they are recalled.

Every time a memory is recalled, it is pieced together – and those pieces change slightly each time. Whatever we've experienced since that event affects the memory as we recall it – and the new version of that memory is then filed. The next time we recall it, we recall the new version – and again, it changes slightly.

Apart from the fact that memories are changing every time we recall them, it is also worth bearing in mind that in CMT therapy, we are changing how memories are held in the subconscious mind, not in the conscious mind. Your conscious mind will always know what really happened, but your subconscious will have the new references.

For more information, and some of the science behind changing childhood memories, refer to the article "Can We Change Adverse Childhood Memories" – which you'll find at the back of this book.

Two Types of Resistance and How to Deal with Them

When attempting to make changes to yourself, your habits, and how you're used to doing things, you will probably experience some resistance. When you start attempting to change childhood memories, it's very common to experience both subconscious and conscious resistance. The subconscious is trying to keep you "safe" by keeping you the same, while consciously, you desire change. The conscious mind is trying to make sense of what you experience.

Subconscious resistance to changing memories will usually come in the form of other memories – proof of whatever it is you're trying to change. In other words, as you try to change one memory of being humiliated, another may come to you. The way to handle this is: Make a note of the memory that has just popped up (just a couple of words to remind you for later), finish changing the one you're currently addressing, and then change the one that popped up during the process.

You'll recognize conscious resistance by the logic and reason. If you find yourself "objecting" to the new memory with arguments like: "But I've never seen her smile" or "But my father left when I was 2 years old" or "But that's not possible because…" – you'll know that's conscious resistance. And the way to address conscious resistance is by using logic and reason. For example: "Yes, but my subconscious doesn't know that. My subconscious can't tell the difference between reality and imagination and can't judge something as unrealistic. It will believe whatever I give it."

Satisfying the Conscious Mind:

We now know that changing childhood memories is the answer to making real changes in all areas of our lives, but, for many people, the conscious mind gets in the way. The subconscious has no ability to tell "right" from "wrong". It also has no ability to use logic or reason, and cannot tell the difference between reality and imagination.

When you see a scary movie, you'll notice that your body goes into the same state it would if the threat were real. Your heart-rate increases; adrenaline is pumped into your system; your palms get sweaty - you experience the "fight-freeze-flight" emergency state. While your conscious mind knows it's just a movie, your subconscious thinks the threat is real, and is prompting your brain to trigger your organs to produce the same stress chemicals they would if you were in real physical danger.

This means that any logical objections to changing memories - for example: "That's not what really happened" "She would never have been like that" "But he never smiled" "But I couldn't have studied what I loved because I've ended up in a completely different career" "But I couldn't have grown up in France because I live in England" "Why should they get away with it" "That's not possible" "That's unrealistic" "That's denial" - and any other arguments along those lines - are coming from the conscious mind, not the subconscious. The subconscious cannot judge in that way. The subconscious only operates according to how it's programmed, based on the proof and evidence it holds (in the form of memories).

So, the solution to this conscious resistance to changing memories is - since the conscious mind uses logic and reason - using logic and reason! And here's how:

Logical Counter-Arguments for Conscious Resistance:

* It doesn't matter because that's over now - it's no longer happening, and it's no longer real now.

* That person isn't here now - they can't fit inside my head - this is just me now.

* This is not really that person in the memory - they can't fit inside my head - this is just a part of me, playing the role of that person; and I'm making peace with that part of me - it's nothing to do with that person.

* My subconscious doesn't know the difference between reality and imagination, and cannot judge something as unrealistic - it will believe whatever I give it.

* I'm reprogramming my subconscious in the same way I would reprogram a computer - I'm simply changing the references. I'm changing the data from limiting and negative, to empowering and beneficial.

* If I really want to improve my life, then this is what I need to do. Just like, if I really want to listen to different music on my phone, I need to replace the old playlist with the songs I want to listen to.

* There are no memory police, and it's my business what I choose to put into my subconscious

* My conscious mind will always know what really happened (just like it knows when I'm watching a movie - that it's just a movie) - I'm only changing the information in my subconscious.

* I am the Boss of Me! I decide what references my subconscious will be referring to from now on!

No Budget, No Limit

There is no limit to the budget inside your mind, and there's no limit to the special effects! And there are no "memory police" – you can create whatever you want inside there! The better you make your new memories, the better the "evidence" you're providing for your subconscious that "proves" the new results you want in your life. So, make it the ideal, make it perfect – there's no limit, and no reason to short-change yourself.

Odille Remmert and Steve Remmert

How to Reprogram
Your Subconscious Mind for
Business Success

Now that you know how the subconscious is programmed in the first place, and how it is determining everything you do with your business, it's time to learn how to change that programming to support the results you want to achieve.

An Experiment

Let's start with this little experiment. Think of your front door. What color is it? If it isn't white, make it white in your mind. Imagine it to be white. Now, make it blue. If you find you can't make it blue, imagine taking out a pot of blue paint – and paint it blue. Now, make it red, now, yellow. Now, add purple flowers to it.

You were probably able to change the color of the

door inside your mind – even though your conscious mind knows it's not that color. The reason this is easier than changing childhood memories, though, is because (presumably) you have no emotional attachment to your front door! It is the emotions that make changing memories more difficult.

When you recall a memory, even though the event is over– it's not happening right now – because your subconscious doesn't know the difference between reality and imagination, it prompts your brain and body to produce the same emotions and feelings they would if it *was* happening now.

Removing the emotional charge to a memory, first, makes it easier to do whatever it takes to change that memory (subconscious reference) to the opposite and positive – giving your subconscious new "evidence" to "prove" the results you want to see in your life.

What is Childhood Memory Transformation (CMT) Therapy?

Childhood Memory Transformation therapy (CMT) is a process for making desired changes to all areas of life by changing the subconscious references in the form of childhood memories.

It comprises seven main techniques:

- FasterEFT
- Generational Childhood Rewriting
- Reverse Visualization
- Transformation Meditations
- Stepping-Stone Memories
- Anchor Memories
- Zero Tolerance

You can use one or more of these techniques – whatever will get you to the end result of: New Childhood Memories (subconscious references).

FasterEFT

FasterEFT (FEFT) is a thinking system and technique created by Robert G. Smith (you can find his website listed under "Resources" at the back of this book).

The main foundation of Childhood Memory Transformation therapy is based on FasterEFT (FEFT) and Robert's technique of "defractionation". Defractionation is the process of creating changes by interrupting focus or "breaking the trance" of the memory. Although you can use anything that will distract your attention, to "defractionate", FEFT Meridian Tapping is one of the most common.

We use the FEFT process to:

1. Find the original memories that are supporting a problem – that are providing the "evidence" that "proves" a belief, issue, habit, or problem.

2. Slow and stop the flow of stress chemicals being pumped into the bloodstream, in order to be able to change the memory.

3. Make changes to specific aspects of a memory when necessary. For example: expressions, actions, sounds, words, colors, and other parts of a memory that are holding it in place.

4. Change memories from negative to the opposite and positive.

5. Establish the new memories by practicing them until the new neural network is established.

The FasterEFT Process – Step-by-Step

Step One

Think of what is bothering you most right now. Pick one thing.

Now, ask yourself these three questions:

1. How do I know this is a problem?
2. How does that feel?
3. Where have I felt that feeling before - and go to your earliest childhood memory of that feeling.

Step Two

Notice how the memory is represented in your mind. Do you see something? Hear something? Feel something? Just notice it.

Now, do whatever it takes to take your focus off it - to distract yourself:

* You can use comedy (watching a funny YouTube video, for example)

* You can sing something

* You can use physical activity (dance, walk, run, household chores)

* You can use "tapping" (see instructions below)

- Whatever will take your focus off the bad feelings and memory in the moment!

FasterEFT - Tapping

Using two fingers, and focusing now on the feeling of your fingers on your skin (or on something else like blue penguins on a trampoline – whatever takes your focus off the bad memory or feeling), gently tap on the following meridian points while saying the phrases:

- Between your eyebrows – "I release and let this go"
- Beside your eye (either eye) – "It's okay to let it go"
- Under your eye – "It's safe to let it go"
- On your collar bone – "I don't need it anymore, and I'm safe as I'm letting it go"
- Grab your wrist, take a deep breath, blow it out, and say "Peace" and go to a peaceful memory. Enjoy that memory for a moment. This is one of the methods of disrupting the body chemistry to break the hold of the bad emotions.

The FasterEFT Process

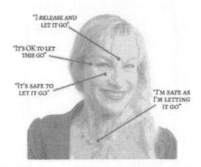

"I RELEASE AND LET IT GO".

"IT'S OK TO LET THIS GO"

"IT'S SAFE TO LET IT GO"

"I'M SAFE AS I'M LETTING IT GO"

1. NOTICE how you KNOW, and FEEL the problem (feeling, image, sound).

2. Now take your focus OFF the problem and TAP on each point, while saying 'LET IT GO'...

3. HOLD YOUR WRIST, take a DEEP BREATH in, blow it out and SAY: "PEACE."

4. Recall a HAPPY MEMORY and enjoy the FEELING of it.

5. Next, go and CHECK the problem again. NOTICE how it is changing.

6. REPEAT the process.

7. CONTINUE the process until you change the FEELING of the memory to positive.

8. Finally, REWRITE the memory to the way you would have liked it to have been (it's your mind- so make it FABULOUS!)

9. REPLAY the new memory at least three times (feel free to add more fabulousness each time)

10. WRITE the new memory in your HAPPY JOURNAL and REPLAY it often.

Step Three

Now, go back to the memory you're addressing, and check to see what's changed. Notice what is still left that doesn't feel good, and then go through Step Two again.

Step Four

Keep doing this, back-and-forth until the feelings and emotions have come down enough for you to be able to change the memory. Make sure that you rewrite it to the opposite and positive.

If you were punished, you want to change it to where you were praised.

If you were scolded, you want to change it to where you were hugged.

If you were beaten, you want to change it to where you are now being taken to Disney World.

Remember: The subconscious doesn't know the difference between reality and imagination; it cannot use logic or reason; it cannot judge something as "unrealistic" and there is no limit to the budget or special effects inside your mind - your subconscious will believe whatever you give it!

And whatever you give it will be providing the new "proof" and "evidence" for who you are, and how the world works - so make it as Fabulous and Empowering as possible!!

Step Five

Now, the most important step: PRACTICE that new memory! Run it through three times in a row, right now. Then, play it through several times a day for the next week.

You can play it through a few times just while brushing your teeth, driving somewhere, or doing household chores.

You don't need to close your eyes, just run it through in your mind as you're doing other things.

Run it through first thing in the morning, when you wake up, and again as you're going to bed at night.

Whenever you feel "triggered" – play your new memory. What you're doing in that moment is

The more you play that new memory, the better the results you'll experience!

Rewriting Generational Childhood

If your parents, and their parents, had grown up differently – had been treated differently as children – they would have turned out to be different people, and different parents. If they had been treated with love, kindness, compassion, respect, and affection, they would have automatically treated those around them the same way they had been treated as children.

They would also have had the foundation for achieving their own dreams and goals, and aspirations. And they would have been happier, healthier, wealthier, more successful, and more fulfilled. And that would have made your childhood very different!

Naturally, we cannot go back and change anyone's actual childhood… but your subconscious doesn't know that! By changing your grandparents' and parents' childhoods in your subconscious (your conscious mind will, of course, still know the original story), you are providing a foundation for your own childhood.

For example: if your parents were highly critical or judgmental, it's because they learned that that's the way to be in the world if you want to survive. There's a wide range of experiences that could have caused this – BUT, it certainly wouldn't be: being treated with kindness, love, compassion, affection, gentle guidance, good role models, encouragement, inspiration, and respect! So, if you imagine what your parents would have been like if they had been raised in that way – you are then giving your subconscious mind different references for your own life.

If you had been raised with love, affection, kindness, compassion, support, enthusiasm, encouragement, gentle guidance, respect, value, attention, security, financial freedom, and the opportunities you desired – you would have automatically created the life you wanted. If your parents had been happy, healthy, emotionally intelligent, financially independent, enthusiastic, fun, fulfilled, doing what they love, you would have followed that blueprint.

Practice imagining your grandparents, and then your parents having happy childhoods. You can follow the description at the back of this book, or watch the video: "Meditation for Rewriting Generational Childhoods" on our YouTube channel (you'll find the link at the back of this book).

The great news is: Your subconscious will believe whatever you give it. All you need to do is: whatever it takes to change those memories (references) to support what you want, rather than what you've had up until now.

Back to Your Future – Reverse Visualization

One of the most effective ways to achieve a goal is to "reverse engineer" it. – to look at the end results you're aiming for, and then work backwards to determine what will get you there. We've discovered that it is also the most effective way to create the changes you want to make in your life.

Decide what you would like – think about what your business will be like once you've achieved what you desire. What kind of success are you aiming for? What's the end goal? What would your ideal life look like?

Now, do whatever it takes to change your childhood memories to where your parents were/did/had that! For example: If you want to be a best-selling author, imagine your mother and/or father with best-sellers.

Use CMT therapy to change your childhood memories (the subconscious references) to where one or both of your parents wrote best-sellers. Imagine them at book-signings, with people lined up, and you're there, with them. Imagine seeing them being interviewed by Oprah.

Remember, your subconscious has no ability to judge something as unrealistic or illogical. It will believe whatever you give it. And what you're doing, as you go through this process is giving your subconscious new references for what is "normal" for you – new references for the "tribe". And that means that, in order to keep you in alignment with your "tribe" your subconscious will start prompting your brain and body to produce chemicals that will give you very different feelings, emotions, impulses – leading you to see yourself and the world differently.

You'll start to come up with ideas, and see opportunities you hadn't before. You'll start to feel inspired to take action you hadn't before, and you'll start to feel differently about your skills and abilities.

Whatever you want right now, change your childhood memories so that your parents had it. Make your parents healthy, wealthy, happy, and successful in your childhood memories. And as you do that, you are programming your "autopilot" with those coordinates! Then, your results will be automatic and effortless!

Transformation Meditations

These are meditations that can help you to rewrite your own childhood. They will also give you an idea of what you're aiming for when changing your memories. Rather than just "better" you want to make your childhood ideal! The better you make it, the better the results you'll experience in your life.

We've included the text version of a Transformation Meditation: "The Story of Your Birth" – at the back of this book. We also have an mp3 audio version of it available on our Patreon site – which you can access, free of charge, whether you're a member of our community there or not. You'll find details for accessing that resource, at the back of this book as well.

Stepping-Stone Memories

"Stepping-stone memory" is a phrase we use to describe an interim memory between the original bad memory, and the ideal new memory.

The Purpose of Stepping-Stone Memories

Stepping-stone memories are, we believe, essential for ensuring that all subconscious references are changed, regarding a particular issue.

For example: If you were bullied when you were 5 years old, and your dad didn't stand up for you, that memory may be providing the following references:

1. My dad doesn't stand up for me - which means I'm worthless.

2. I was bullied - which means I'm weak.

You could change the memory to where your dad did stand up for you. And that's great - that means that your subconscious now has a reference that your dad stood up for you, and perhaps that will contribute towards a structure for "I'm worthy".

But, if the memory remains that way, the subconscious still has a reference that you were bullied

- so that is still providing the "evidence" for the belief: "I'm weak".

If, on the other hand, you change the memory directly to where weren't bullied in the first place, that's great - and your subconscious will no longer have that reference providing "evidence" that you're weak... but it also won't have a reference for your dad standing up for you.

Note:

Your conscious mind is able to reason: If I wasn't bullied in the first place, then there was no need for my dad to stand up for me. However, remember that your subconscious does not use reason or logic. And the information collected and stored – from the experience of your dad not standing up from you – is separate data that is supporting a different (probably more than one) belief, and will be connected to other "evidence" that combine to support that belief.

The answer? Stepping-stone memories!

How to Use Stepping-Stone Memories:

Using the example above...

1. First, use FEFT to change the memory to where you were bullied AND your dad stood up for you and protected you. This will change that reference in your subconscious - giving it proof that you are worthy.

2. Practice that stepping-stone memory three times in a row.

3. Now, use FEFT again, to change the stepping-stone memory to where you weren't bullied in the first place! You were never bullied. You were popular; and the "bullies" are now friends and admirers in your new memory. You see your dad with you, proud of you, and you are having fun doing stuff together. This is now your final new memory.

4. Practice that new memory three times in a row.

5. Write that new memory down, and practice it 12 times a day for the first week.

Using More than One Stepping-Stone Memory

You can use more than one stepping-stone memory - for example: if your father left when you were 3 years old, and then came back when you were 10 years old, and was abusive, and your mother never protected you - here are example stepping-stone memories you could create the following, using Faster EFT:

1st Stepping-Stone Memory:
When your father came back and was abusive, your mother protected you.

2nd Stepping-Stone Memory:
Now, when your father comes back, he's not abusive - he's loving and affectionate, so happy to see

you, and tells you how much he missed you.

<u>New Memory</u>:
Now, change that to where your father never left in the first place.

Using these stepping-stone memories means you are changing multiple references in your subconscious along the way, with each step, until you arrive at the ideal new, positive and empowering reference - the final New Memory.

Points to Bear in Mind

As you change memories, whether they're stepping-stone or the ultimate new memory, keep reminding yourself:

* The subconscious cannot tell the difference between reality and imagination
* The subconscious cannot judge something as unrealistic
* The subconscious cannot use logic or reason

- which means the subconscious will believe whatever you give it. It's only your conscious mind that knows the difference. Just like your conscious mind knows that a scary movie is just a movie, but your subconscious triggers the "fight-freeze-flight" emergency state in your body while you're watching - as if the threat is real!

Anchor Memories

When you find that a memory is not changing – or an aspect of it is not changing – it may be because there is an "anchor memory" holding it in place. In this case, all you need to do is change the anchor memory, and then see if you can change that memory again. You can find anchor memories through this process:

Notice what happens when you try to change the memory (or try to play the new memory). It may be that a piece of the old memory remains, or that a certain feeling comes up that prevents you from changing it (or playing the new one) – just notice what's there.

Now, ask yourself if that reminds you of anything (and it may seem to have nothing to do with the memory you're working on – remember, the subconscious doesn't use logic or reason, so it often makes connections that may seem completely illogical or unreasonable to the conscious mind).

If a memory comes up (even if it appears to be "random" and have nothing to do with the current memory you're working on) change that one before going back to the one you were working on and seeing if you can change it (or play the new one) now.

Note: There may be more than one anchor; so, if you go through the above steps, and find you still can't change the memory or play the new one, go through

Zero Tolerance

The purpose of Zero Tolerance is to ensure that the emotions don't become overwhelming. When we don't address something right away, in the moment, the emotions build and build because the conscious mind continues to find reasons for the feelings, and that perpetuates the feelings (as the limbic system responds to the thoughts with more of the matching chemicals) - this makes it harder to address that issue, and sometimes even impossible.

1. The subconscious prompts the brain to trigger the organs to produce chemicals.

2. The chemicals cause sensations and feelings.

3. The conscious mind automatically looks for reasons for the sensations and feelings.

4. The thoughts about the reasons create more of those chemicals....

And so, it becomes a vicious circle - with increasing amounts of stress chemicals being pumped into the bloodstream, intensifying the effects of the fight-freeze-flight response. This makes it harder and harder for the conscious mind to see reason (with the prefrontal cortex of the brain shut down in this state), and therefore you are less likely to use FEFT to address the issue, and are more likely to go with old coping skills, and repeat old patterns of emotional and physical behavior.

How to Use Zero Tolerance

1. **If the emotions are not overwhelming**, and you have time in the moment, notice the feeling, and then think back to where you've felt it before (earliest, if possible), remembering that it may not be the same circumstances but will be the same feeling. For example, the early memory of guilt may not be to do with missing a deadline - it could be something completely different, but will be the same feeling.

2. **If the emotions are too strong**, do whatever it takes in the moment to pull yourself out of them - tapping may be enough, but if not, then do something else that will pull you out: physical exercise; music; watching or listening to something funny; etc. Then go back to it later, when the emotions aren't so strong. But make sure that you do go back to it - that will make the difference between just burying it inside you by distraction, and actually getting rid of it.

3. **If you can't think of a memory** in that moment, just notice what's there. In this case, just notice how the guilt feels, where in your body you feel it, and if there are any words or phrases that come to you. Then, tap on that until it flips. While you're tapping, you may find that memories do come up, but if not, don't worry - just keep tapping until it flips. Your subconscious is still doing the work in the background!

4. **If you can think of a memory**, but don't have time to address it in that moment, then make a note of the memory (just a word or two to remind you later) - I would recommend putting an alarm in your phone for later when you'll have some time. Then, do Option 3 above (notice and tap until the feeling flips). Later, when your alarm goes off and you have time, address that original memory, and change it to the opposite and positive.

The Key Point About Zero Tolerance:

Catching the negative state as soon as it starts, and doing whatever it takes to pull yourself out of it. It's zero tolerance for anything negative – zero tolerance for any negative thoughts or feelings, no matter how small or apparently insignificant.

Think of it this way: The longer you allow yourself to feel any kind of negative feeling – no matter how minor it may seem, the more stress chemicals are being pumped into your bloodstream, and the stronger that negative state will become, over time.

Imagine it as a tap running, flooding your bloodstream with stress chemicals. As soon as you notice the tap is running, you need to switch it off. If you don't, every moment you leave it running, increasing levels of stress chemicals are entering your bloodstream – making it more difficult to dilute and dissipate them when the emotions become stronger. The earlier you turn off that tap, and "turn on" the endorphins (feel-good chemicals), by turning your focus to happy, funny, fun stuff, or even just thinking of things you're grateful for – the easier and quicker it will be to reduce the levels of stress chemicals and move forward in a more productive, creative, effective way.

Step-by-Step Process to Reprogram Your Subconscious Mind for Business Success

Follow these steps to start changing the subconscious references that are determining your current business results. If you get stuck, refer to the information in the rest of this book, or reach out to us for help through our Patreon Community here: www.patreon.com/ftsr

Warning:

If you have trauma memories, or anything else in which the emotions are higher than you feel you can handle on your own, it is important to seek help from a certified practitioner.

We both offer one-to-one sessions for those who need them (you can find the link to more information on these, at the back of this book). You can also find other certified FasterEFT practitioners on the official FasterEFT website (link at the back of this book). We highly recommend you work with a certified practitioner for any trauma.

Step One:

Ask yourself these three questions:

1. How do I know I have a problem (or how do I know this is a problem)?

For example: I feel overwhelmed and can't prioritize; or I don't have enough time; or I feel uncomfortable charging people.

2. How does that feel?

For example: I feel frustrated; anxious; worried; like I'm trapped; like my hands are tied

3. **What's my earliest childhood memory of feeling that same feeling?** *(note: it may not be the same topic – for example money or not enough time - but will be the same feeling)*

For example: My parents' expectations; or not being allowed to play sport; or being ill as a child; or being punished by the 2nd grade teacher.

Make a note of the earliest memories of this feeling, and put the approximate age you were, in brackets.

Here are a few examples:

Example One:

1. How do I know I have a problem?

I don't believe anyone will want to buy my products.

2. How does that feel?

It feels like I'm not good enough.

3. What's my earliest memory of that same feeling?

My mother always preferred my brother to me.

Earliest Memory:

My brother and me fighting and my mother punishing me and not him, even though he started the fight (6 yrs)

Example Two:

1. How do I know I have a problem?

People just don't seem to book with me, no matter how much marketing or advertising I do.

2. How does that feel?

I feel hopeless and helpless.

3. What's my earliest memory of that same feeling?

Almost drowning in the lake (4yrs)

Example Three:

1. How do I know I have a problem?

Every time I start to get ahead, something happens to set me back again.

2. How does that feel?

I feel frustrated and trapped.

3. What's my earliest memory of that same feeling?

The same feeling I had with my abusive father.

Earliest Memory:

Earliest memory of being whipped with the belt (8yrs)

Example Four:

1. How do I know I have a problem?

I can't do a blog because I can't write.

2. How does that feel?

I feel stupid.

3. What's my earliest memory of that same feeling?

Teacher humiliating me in 5th grade. (10 yrs.)

Example Five:

1. How do I know I have a problem?

I can't do social media because I don't know what to say – I don't know what to post.

2. How does that feel?

I feel frozen.

3. What's my earliest memory of that same feeling?

Bullies attacking me at school (11 yrs.)

<u>Example Six:</u>

1. How do I know I have a problem?

I just can't get motivated to do what I know I need to do.

2. How does that feel?

I feel depressed.

3. What's my earliest memory of that same feeling?

Seeing my mother depressed.

Earliest Memory:

Coming home from school and seeing my mother crying. (7yrs)

<u>Example Seven:</u>

1. How do I know I have a problem?

I never seem to have enough time to do everything I need to do to move my business forward.

2. How does that feel?

I feel overwhelmed – like a heavy weight on my chest.

3. What's my earliest memory of that same feeling?

The feeling of being held down when my brother bullied me. (8 yrs.)

Step Two:

Now ask yourself these questions:

1. **Who else do I know who had this problem (or something similar, or similar feelings) when I was a child?** (Make a note of your earliest bad memory of that person)

For example: My father was always talking about being overwhelmed:

Memory: Dad missing my birthday party because he was working. (6yrs)

2. **If this problem was a person, who would it be?** (Make a note of your earliest bad memory of that person)

For example: It would be my mother because she

was never there for me, just like money is never there for me.

Memory: Mom forgetting to pick me up from school, and then being angry with me. (8yrs)

Here are a few examples:

1. **Who else do I know who had this problem (or something similar, or similar feelings) when I was a child?**

My aunt had depression. I remember my parents talking about how she stopped going out and would sit on the couch all day, watching TV.

Memory: Imagining my aunt on the couch never moving – it felt really depressing. (About 11 yrs)

(Note: being told about something is as relevant as a memory of something you experienced personally – bearing in mind your subconscious doesn't know the difference between reality and imagination, it can create memories that seem real, just from something you heard about. You can change the memory itself (the picture,

feeling etc.) <u>and</u> the memory of being told about it).

2. **If this problem was a person, who would it be?**

My cousin, Jim – because he rejected me, just like potential clients or collaborators are rejecting me.

Memory: Jim making fun of me in front of his friends when I asked if I could play with them. (5yrs)

1. **Who else do I know who had this problem (or something similar, or similar feelings) when I was a child?**

My grandmother was always talking about how our family was "cursed" and no-one ever did anything for us, and everyone always betrayed us.

Memory: No specific memory – just an overall "knowing" that that's what she said. (Age – ever-since I can remember)

2. **If this problem was a person, who would it be?**

The neighbor of the first house we lived in because he was always mean to us, and complained about us walking on his grass - just like it seems I keep ending up working with mean people who complain about spending money.

Memory: Can't remember the earliest time it happened, but the earliest I can remember is when he chased us down the road brandishing a shovel. (10 yrs.)

Step Three:

Now, ask yourself the following:

- What is my earliest bad memory of my mother?

- What is my earliest bad memory of my father?

- What is my earliest bad school memory?

- What is my earliest bad memory of other significant people from my childhood (grandparents, siblings, neighbors, etc.)

Make a note of these memories, with the approximate age in brackets.

Step Four:

Next, ask yourself:

If my business were to succeed in the way I want it to, what <u>bad</u> things would happen?

Now, this may seem like an absurd question, but it can very often lead to memories that your subconscious is referring to as "proof" that you would be in "danger" if you succeeded in making the changes you want to make.

Then, ask yourself:

- How do I know that will happen?

- What proof do I have (or past experiences)?

- Where did I learn about that or hear about it?

- What's my earliest memory of it?

<u>For example</u>:

If my business were to succeed in the way I want it to, what <u>bad</u> things would happen?

If my business succeeds, I won't have an excuse to miss social events because I won't have to work so hard.

- My friends always complain that I work too hard and don't have time with them, but I don't like going out with them anymore, since Jenny joined them.

- It feels the same as when I was in 3rd grade, and my best friend found a new friend and snubbed me in front of everyone at lunchtime. So, I tried to make sure I was always busy with something during lunch-time. (8yrs)

Or:

If my business were to succeed in the way I want it to, what <u>bad</u> things would happen?

If I get more customers, I'll feel overwhelmed because I don't know if I have enough content.

- When I think about doing more, I feel tired at the thought of it.

- In my previous work, it felt like a never-ending load.

- I had to help my mother clean the house, and whenever my dad had friends over, it felt like there was a never-ending job of cleaning up when I really wanted to be outside, playing with my friends. (10 yrs.)

Now, put your list of early childhood memories, that you've found from these steps, in order of age.

For example:

- Almost drowning in the lake (4yrs)

- Jim making fun of me in front of his friends when I asked if I could play with them. (5yrs)

- Hearing about a kid in school who died (5yrs)

- My mother spanking me with the belt (8yrs)

- My best friend snubbing me at lunch time (8yrs)

- My cat died (9yrs)

- My father leaving us (10 yrs.)

- Imagining my aunt on the couch never moving – it felt really depressing. (About 11 yrs.)

Step Five:

Starting with your earliest memory:

1. Notice what's there when you think about this memory — notice how you know it happened — is there a picture? A feeling? Any sound? Just a knowing? Notice whatever's there. If there's an emotion or feeling, start with that.

2. Now, take your focus off it, and do one or more of the following:

-   Tap — making sure you're keeping your focus off the memory or feeling while you're tapping — Follow the instructions in the sub-chapter: FasterEFT.

-   Press "play" on a funny video on YouTube (babies laughing is a good one) and watch until you laugh or smile, then press "Pause"

-   Press "play" on one of your favorite songs, and either sing along or dance to it until you're smiling, then press "Pause"

3. Now, go back <u>very briefly</u> and notice if that feeling in the memory is still there – if it is, notice how strong it is. <u>Note</u>: Don't stay in the feeling – just <u>very briefly</u> notice – it shouldn't take you more than a few seconds.

4. Tap or press "play" again.

5. Keep doing this back-and-forth until you're able to change the feeling and create a new memory

6. Rewrite this now – and make it the ideal, rather than just "better than it was" – for example: Instead of being punished, your parent spoke with you, reasoned with you, explained things to you, and guided you with kindness and compassion – and asked for your side of the story, wanting to understand you. Remember – your subconscious doesn't use logic or reason,

and will believe whatever you give it. So, choose something that feels good. You could use this memory as a stepping-stone. memory – and then change it to – <u>you never did anything wrong in the first place</u>.

Here's another example of changing a memory to the ideal: Instead of growing up without your father or mother – both of your parents had a bedtime ritual where they would read to you every night. They would get into bed with you, one either side, and would read to you as you fell into a safe, peaceful sleep.

Once you were asleep, they would watch you for a little while, marveling at how amazing you are, and how much they loved you. They had had no idea, before you were born, that it was possible to love someone this much. They would each kiss you gently, and then carefully climb out of the bed, switching off the lamp, and leaving the little night light on, closing the door, quietly, and leaving you sleeping soundly.

In the morning, as you woke, you would hear them chatting and laughing in the kitchen as they prepared breakfast together. Their faces always lit up when you entered the room, and they regularly told you how much they loved you, how proud they were of you, and how grateful they were to have you as their child. *(Remember, if you find yourself objecting: "But my dad left" or "But my mother worked two jobs" or "I can't imagine my father or mother kissing me or reading to me" – remind yourself, your subconscious doesn't use reason or logic and will believe whatever you give it!)*

Another one is: Your parents were both successful business people. Money came easily to them, and they were always happy, relaxed, and fun. Their income came from doing what they loved, and they taught you everything they knew about how to be successful in business (you don't need to go into the details of that – you just need to "remember" the feeling of the connection with them – how lovely it felt to spend time with your parents as they involved you in the business/s they loved so much) – and clients/customers flocked to them as they were so popular and so loved!

Can you imagine how powerful and empowering those new subconscious references will be?

That is the new "evidence" we want to give your subconscious – to prove that you are safe, worthy, loved, powerful, confident, healthy, happy, successful, abundant, and that it is safe to feel good, have a fun, enjoyable, abundant, relaxed life, and do whatever you want to do!

7. Now, play that new memory through three times in a row, grab your wrist, take a deep breath, blow it out and say "Peace"

3. Write down that new memory, and play it 12 times a day for the next week – this is a crucial step, and will make all the difference to your results! 12 times sounds like a lot, but you can play your new memories through three or four times just while

brushing your teeth! It doesn't need to take long, and you don't need to close your eyes to do it – you can run through them while you're driving somewhere or doing household chores, or working out in the gym. Make this a top priority in your day since it is what will make the difference to your success!

Now, once you've done that, move on to the next memory on your list (next earliest age), and do the same as above.

You're aiming to change your whole childhood to wonderful – bearing in mind your subconscious won't know the difference between reality and imagination – you will be giving your subconscious NEW references – references that are empowering and positive and that mean you are safe, loved, worthy, respected, happy, healthy, abundant, deserving, and everything else you want to be.

<u>Note</u>:

If you have trouble changing a memory, or playing a new memory (for example, the old memory keeps coming back) – use the Anchor Memory Technique – or reach out to us through our Patreon Community, for help.

Step Six:

Use the Generational Childhood Rewriting process and the Transformation Meditation to continue to improve your results.

Odille Remmert and Steve Remmert

Conclusion

Here are the key points to keep in mind:

1. No matter what is going on for you right now – no matter what your challenges are with your business right now, the way you are experiencing them is determined by the references held in your subconscious in the form of childhood memories.

2. Changing those memories will automatically result in a change in your current and future experiences – because your subconscious will be referring to different "evidence" – evidence that you are worthy, creative, loved, safe, secure, clever, intelligent, good, talented, valuable, respected, confident, interesting, wonderful, healthy, energetic, inspired, productive, a leader, charismatic… and everything else that you want to be.

3. Memories are not real - the event is not happening now, what you're experiencing in

your mind is just neurons firing in a specific sequence, and chemicals being pumped into your blood stream, creating sensations, feelings, emotions, and impulses. This means you can change them.

4. Your subconscious cannot tell the difference between reality and imagination, cannot use logic or reason, and cannot judge something as unrealistic. It will believe whatever you give it. So, although you will still know, consciously, what happened, as long as you practice the new memories to establish that new neural network, your subconscious will believe the new "evidence" and use that as the new reference.

5. There are no memory police, and there's no limit to the budget or special effects inside your subconscious – you can create whatever you want in there. And the more amazing you make your new memories, the better the results you'll see in your business. You can even add celebrities and fictional characters – your subconscious won't know that's not possible!

6. Don't give up! If you come across resistance, use the resources in this eBook, or reach out to us through our Patreon Community! Don't stop until you get what you want.

7. When in doubt – when you're not sure which

memories to change, or you can't find any memories - just rewrite your whole childhood. Start from birth, and change the lot, using the processes above. If you find that difficult, use the Generational Childhood Rewriting technique to change your grandparents' and parents' childhoods – if they'd been raised differently, they would have been different parents… and your childhood would have been different.

The Bottom Line:

If you really want success in your business, you need to change your childhood memories to support that reality. Just as, if you wanted to change the direction in which an airplane was headed, you'd need to change the coordinates in the autopilot. If you wanted to change the words that are on a document that's coming out of your printer, you'd need to change them in the document on your computer – then you'd automatically get the document with the changes coming out of the printer!

Change the Programs, Change Your Business.

Odille Remmert and Steve Remmert

References and Resources

Rewriting Generational Childhoods
See the script at the back of this book.
You can also find the video guide on our YouTube Channel: Fast-Track Subconscious Reprogramming.

Transformation Meditation – The Story of Your Birth
See the script at the back of this book

Watch the Videos on Our YouTube Channel:
Fast-Track Subconscious Reprogramming

Join Our Community on Patreon for Daily Podcasts, Live Sessions and Videos:
Get your questions answered through our community forum, and follow along with live group sessions. **www.patreon.com/ftsr**

One-to-One Skype/ Zoom Sessions:
We do a limited number of private one-to-one sessions as we prefer to empower people to learn to make the changes for themselves. However, there are times we all need a little one-to-one help, especially with trauma: **www.subconscious-reprogramming.com**

FasterEFT by Robert G. Smith – Official Website:
www.fastereft.com

Our Website:
www.subconscious-reprogramming.com

Scientific References:
Can We Change Adverse Childhood Memories?
bit.ly/ace-article

Can We Change Adverse Childhood Memories?

The ACE study highlighted the problem. Now What?

The ACE (Adverse Childhood Experiences) study showed that adverse experiences during childhood significantly affect the adult.

Events that include (but are not limited to) physical, emotional, and sexual abuse; physical and emotional neglect; parental separation or divorce; and violence within the household, have been found to impact the experiences of the adult that child becomes.

ACEs have been connected to: social, emotional, and cognitive impairment; the adoption of health-risk behaviors; disability; disease; social problems; unemployment; poverty; and early death.

The data gathered from the ACE study has provided a powerful insight into the connection between childhood adverse experiences and challenges in adulthood.

This has led to a focus on child protection services, awareness in schools, and a drive to help parents to provide a safer, calmer, more secure and nurturing environment for their offspring.

The goal is to lower the risk of problems in the adult, by ensuring reduced adverse experiences in the child. And that is an essential step in improving the overall statistics, moving forward.

But what about those of us who've "missed that boat"? What about adults around the world, who are currently suffering the consequences of ACEs, and— until time travel is invented—are "stuck" with our baggage?

How are ACEs Affecting Adults?

It seems clear that the developing brain is affected by adverse childhood experiences, but how?

We now know that, not only is the brain not "hard-wired" by adulthood, but it is constantly changing.

Every time we learn new information, process information we already know differently, or encounter new experiences, the brain changes.

This means that, although a large part of the connection between ACEs and adverse experiences in adults may be the interruption to development in the brain due to the high levels of stress in childhood, it's possible there's more.

Results from a study by Dr. Tazu Aoki and Dr. Hitoshi Okamoto from the Laboratory for Developmental Gene Regulation, indicate that: from birth, memories form the foundation of who we are and how the world around us works. We learn our identity and how to operate and survive in our environment, by interpreting and storing "facts", "proof", and "evidence" from experiences.

The Cerebellum, Conditioned Responses, and Memory

According to eye-blink conditioning research carried out by David A. McCormick, et al. at Stanford University, California, in 1981, the cerebellum is involved in conditioned associative learning.

John E. Desmond, M.S., Ph.D. using neuroimaging in his verb-for-noun generation task, found that, while the *search* for the word activated the frontal lobe, the *selection* of which word the subject would use, activated the cerebellum.

The cerebellum is connected to the prefrontal cortex, the posterior parietal region, and the temporal lobe through a series of pathways through the cerebral cortex.

In addition to this: as discovered by Christophe Habas, et al. in their research into cerebellar contributions to intrinsic connectivity networks, the intense activity in the default mode network of the cerebellum during periods of physical inactivity, while imagining the past, the present and the future, indicates that the cerebellum is involved in creative thought, in addition to motor function.

Putting all of this together...

Is it possible that the cerebellum is constantly referring to information stored throughout the brain, in response to conditioned learning, in the form of memories, and then prompting responses in the limbic system?

This could mean that the cerebellum, is controlling automated emotions, sensations and impulses through the body, based on conditioned learning from stored information in the form of childhood memories.

Memory Formation and Recall

While science still has a long way to go in understanding the full details of memory formation and recall, we do know, so far, that memories are not permanent, accurate, or complete.

In fact, according to many recent studies, and an article published in The Journal of Neuroscience: JNeurosci, on August, 29th, 2012 by Bridge and Paller, it seems that memories are reconstructed every time they're recalled. Taking into account the findings of the ACE study, both prototype and exemplar memory will be affected by childhood experiences.

Every childhood experience, presumably, would contribute to the formation of memory category — resulting in each individual's perception of reality being dependent on their childhood experiences.

Neuroplasticity may mean we can change the past — at least, in the way it's represented in memories.

Optogenetics — Generation of a Synthetic Memory Trace (in Mice)

In January 2012, the American Association for the Advancement of Science published an article detailing results of research in which scientists were able to replace fear memories, and create false memories, in mice.

This was achieved by manually manipulating neurons. But do we really need to wait for science, medicine, and technology to develop drugs or gadgets that can be safely used by humans before we have the ability to replace traumatic memories with benign (or even happy) ones?

Is it possible that, considering the human brain's remarkable ability to change itself—along with the fact that the unconscious brain and body seem unable to determine between imagination and reality—we already have the power to create results, without external intervention?

Is it Wrong to Change Memories?

As we now know, memories are not only inaccurate, but actually change every time they are recalled.

In other words, when you recall an event—as you recall it, it is pieced together, and affected by experiences you've had since that event (and the changes that have occurred in your brain since that event).

Then, when you "file" that memory again, you file the new, revised memory.

PTSD and Changing Memories

Memory reconsolidation has proven to be successful, in some cases, for the treatment of post-traumatic stress disorder (PTSD).

However, it is inconsistent and unreliable. Is it possible that the reason for this is that the treatment is targeting the memories of the traumatic events that appear to have caused the PTSD, and not the original references provided by childhood experiences (primary prototype and exemplar memories)?

Excerpt from Article on Medium.com: http://bit.ly/ace-article

Rewriting Generational Childhood – Sample Script

Use this as a sample script – and repeat it for each of your grandparents, and your parents. Fill in the blank with your grandparent's or parent's name.

Imagine _____ as a very small child. Imagine him/her being raised by parents who absolutely adore him/her. They treat him/her with love, compassion, kindness, respect, guidance, and enthusiasm. His/Her parents take time out to spend playing with him/her, and they listen and make eye contact whenever he/she speaks. They appreciate him/her, and their faces light up whenever he/she enters the room. Both parents are financially independent and secure, and the home is full of peace, love, abundance, and security. They live in a wonderful place, with plenty of abundance, and safety.

Now, imagine the kind of child that little one would have grown into with that kind of loving support. And imagine how he/she would have done at school. Able to concentrate because of feeling secure, safe, loved, and supported at home; popular because of feeling confident, being compassionate and kind, fun, and intelligent. And imagine the kind of teenager he/she would have grown into – with that kind of secure, stable, loving, affectionate and abundant upbringing. He/she has everything he/she needs, and complete support from his/her parents.

Now, imagine the kind of man/woman he/she would have grown into – with that kind of foundation and background. Happy, healthy, successful, financially secure, fun, kind, compassionate, respectful, affectionate, loving, joyful. And now, image the kind of father/mother he/she would have become. He/she would have been able to treat their child with the same love, affection, kindness, compassion, and respect that he/she was treated with.

Transformation Meditation – The Story of Your Birth

Read this story through, imagining it in whatever way comes naturally to you.

When you experience any kind of resistance, stop reading for a moment, and address it:

1.   If it is logical objection – for example: "My father wasn't there when I was born"; or "It was a difficult birth" or "My parents had no money for a separate nursery" – that is Conscious Resistance. In this case, use logic and reason to address it – for example: "It doesn't matter because my subconscious doesn't know the difference, and will believe whatever I give it" or "I can't change the original event – that's over now – but I can change how my subconscious holds it" or "There are no memory police. I can change this to whatever I want it to have been – and the better I make it in my imagination, the better the new

references I'm giving my subconscious (so, why not make it ideal!)... and the better the results I'll experience in my life today"

2. If the resistance is in the form of other memories coming up, that simply means that your subconscious has "proof" that contradicts this new memory – and all you need to do is change that "proof"! Make a note of the memories that come up (just one or two words to remind you of them), and then use FEFT to change each one to the opposite and positive. As you do this, you are giving your subconscious "proof" that this new memory is the real story – which will provide the foundation for the changes you want to see in your life, moving forward.

The Story of Your Birth

Your parents were so excited when they found out they were expecting you! They spent hours browsing baby stores together, choosing the best, cutest, cuddliest toys, accessories, and clothes.

They loved preparing the nursery – designing it to be just perfect. With gorgeous colors, pictures, toys, and furniture. They couldn't wait for your arrival. They were so much in love, and you were the perfect expression of that love.

Both your parents spent time reading and learning as much as they could about caring for a baby, and daydreaming about how wonderful it was going to be to have you with them.

The first time they went for a scan, and heard your heartbeat, your dad was so overwhelmed by the moment that he had tears in his eyes, and as he and your mother gazed at each other, their hearts were filled with the love between them and their love for you.

Your dad put the print-out of the first scanned picture of you, in his wallet, and it is still there now. He had to have it laminated to protect it over the years.

The day you were born, was a beautiful day, and your mom was feeling calm, but excited to finally have you in her arms. That morning, she and your dad stood in the nursery, looking at the crib and the tiny clothes, and feeling the anticipation and excitement that they would finally have the baby to go with all of these things!

It as a remarkably quick and easy birth. In fact, the staff mentioned that it was one of the easiest and smoothest births they'd ever attended. Your mom was tired, but happy and grateful to be holding you, her perfect, precious baby, in her arms. Your dad, having been with your mom, holding her hand and encouraging her through the labor, gazed down at his precious wife and newborn baby, feeling his heart swell with love, pride, and gratitude. Holding you for the first time, his heart made a promise to you that he would always be there for you; always protect you; and always make sure that you knew how much he loved you. A promise he was able to keep as you grew into the amazing person he still treasures and loves so much today.

You can find the mp3 audio recording of this guide on our Patreon site. It is available, free of charge – whether you are a member of our community or not.

Go to: **www.patreon.com/ftsr**

- And click on "Transformation Meditations" in the tags, on the left side of the page.

Odille Remmert and Steve Remmert

Notes:

Odille Remmert and Steve Remmert

Odille Remmert and Steve Remmert

Movie

Spring Summer Fall Winter and Spring

The Act of Killing

The Edukators

Per fume : The Story of a murder.

Le Grande Bellezza

Die Welle
Das Experiment } Social Structure

Gods Must be Crazy

Gattaca

Before Midnight

Ladri di bicidette

Samsara (not the doc) ✗

Solaris

Limitless

Batoru Rowaiaru

The Perverts Guide to Ideology

Das Leben Der Anderen - The lives of others

Adams aebler